BRUCE HORNSBY

ANTHOLOGY

FOREWORD

This collection of 40 songs represents the first seven years of songwriting for our records, with collaboration with Don Henley for his record, "The End of the Innocence" included (mostly because I'm proud of it). The transcriptions, especially the last three records should be almost totally correct and complete, as I have edited them myself over the years to make sure that the sheet music gave a satisfying replication of the sound of the records. If the sound seems less full than the records, as, for instance, in the case of "The Way It Is", try adding a tenth in the bass if you can reach it, and also a fifth for a 1-5-10 fuller sounding bass chord (unless the register of the bass is too low; then, just use fifths or octaves). On the first three records, mostly just the piano solos were transcribed, but in the music for the fourth record "Harbor Lights" you will find transcriptions of several guitar solos by Pat Metheny and Jerry Garcia. I'd like to thank the transcribers who have done a painstakingly thorough and good job over the years, and I hope you enjoy playing the songs.

We'll see you around somewhere in your town,

Thanks,

Bruce R. Hornsby

Bruce R. Hornsby

P.S. Any questions? Just write to:
Bruce Hornsby
P.O. Box 3545
Williamsburg, VA 23187

CONTENTS

On The Western Skyline

Words and Music by
B.R. HORNSBY and JOHN HORNSBY

A-bout this time of_ eve — ning out by the bay_ they
roof-tops sag on_ Sec-ond Street. Bach - e-lor's quar - ters,_
Give me shin - y_ Ca-dil - lac and close your eyes_

EVERY LITTLE KISS

Words by
B.R. HORNSBY

Way out
Ev - 'ry - bod - y here's a num-

14

MANDOLIN RAIN

Words and Music by
B.R. HORNSBY and JOHN HORNSBY

20

21

THE LONG RACE

Words and Music by
B.R. HORNSBY and JOHN HORNSBY

twi - light dis - tance on____ the bay long____ my
work so____ hard all day____ show-ing

mind sees____ you run - ning____ through the marsh - land.
me what_you want you go af - ter.

1. All of these years____ I've been wait-ing for you through high tides and low tides____
2.3. All of these years____ I've been push-ing so hard through high tides and low tides____

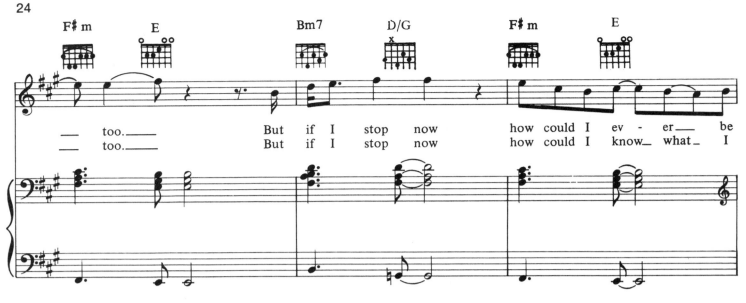

But if I stop now how could I ev - er be
But if I stop now how could I know__ what I

with you?}
could do?}

Oh,_____ it's a long, long__ race.__

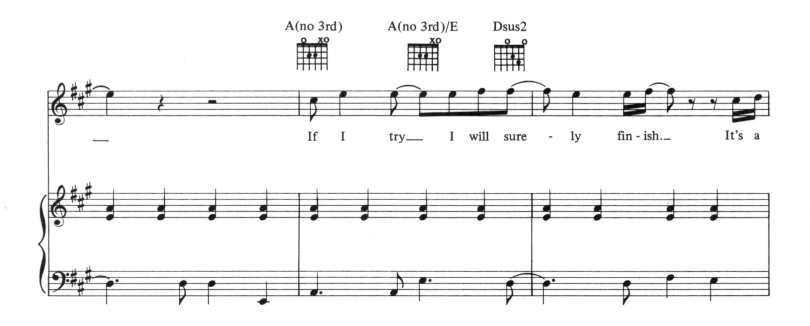

If I try__ I will sure - ly fin - ish.__ It's a

long, long_____ race._____

If I try_____ I will sure - ly fin - ish._____ It's a

The Way It Is

Words and Music by
B.R. HORNSBY

Down The Road Tonight

Words and Music by
B.R. HORNSBY and JOHN HORNSBY

2.

Csus2 G D Gsus2 G Em7sus4 Em7 Gsus2 G C G/C D/E Em7 Am7 G/A

road to - night.—

Cadd9 G D Gsus2 G Em7sus4 Em7 Gsus2 G C G/C D/E Em7 Am7 G/A

Csus2 G Em D Cadd9 Am7 D/F♯

There were mov - ies in the par - lor,— they were deal - in' one-eyed jacks._____ And

D.S. al Coda

Em7 Am7 Cadd9 D C/E D/F♯

when I said I loved_ her,_ she said, "Just_ keep a - com - ing back."

THE WILD FRONTIER

Moderately bright

Words and Music by
B.R. HORNSBY and JOHN HORNSBY

tier.

in the wild. . .

in the wild fron - tier.

(Drums go wild. . .)

Repeat and fade

The River Runs Low

Words and Music
B.R. HORNSBY and JOHN HORNSBY

THE RED PLAINS

Words and Music by
B.R. HORNSBY and JOHN HORNSBY

50

THE VALLEY ROAD

Words and Music by
B.R. HORNSBY and JOHN HORNSBY

THE SHOW GOES ON

Words and Music by
B.R. HORNSBY

What's the long_ face?_ · What's all _ the cry - in' for?_ Did -n't you ex -pect_ it
Some say she's_ al -right, some say_ she'll nev - er learn._ Some rush in - to_ things,

Repeat and fade

TILL THE DREAMING'S DONE

Words and Music by
B.R. HORNSBY

72

I Will Walk With You

Words and Music by
B.R. HORNSBY and JOHN HORNSBY

* During guitar solo, piano plays ad lib following chord changes.
(Note chord substitution in 3rd and 11th bars.)

Defenders Of The Flag

Words and Music by
B.R. HORNSBY and JOHN HORNSBY

Well, the flag. ___

82

LOOK OUT ANY WINDOW

Words and Music by
B.R. HORNSBY and JOHN HORNSBY

88

THE OLD PLAYGROUND

Moderately fast, in 2

Words and Music by
B.R. HORNSBY and JOHN HORNSBY

The old

94

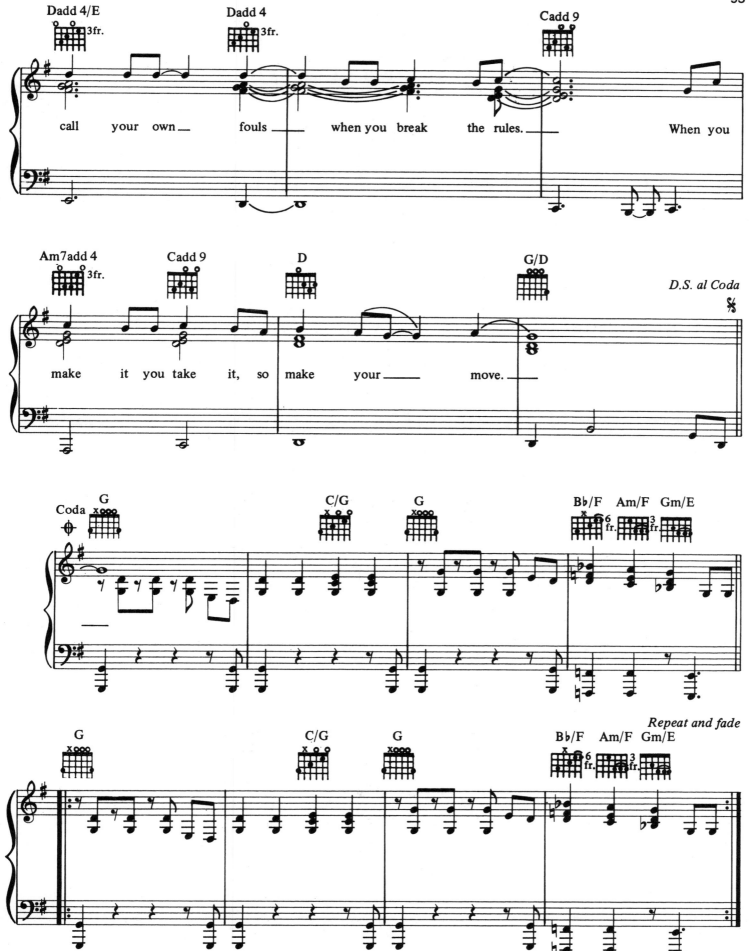

THE ROAD NOT TAKEN

Words and Music by
B.R. HORNSBY

Coda

Oh, I go down the road not tak - en _____ a - gain.

Double time feel

Repeat and fade

JACOB'S LADDER

Words and Music by
B.R. HORNSBY and JOHN HORNSBY

I met a fan danc - er down in south side Bir - ming - ham.__

Com - in' o - ver the air - waves, the man says I'm o - ver - due.__

104

Across The River

Words and Music by
B.R. HORNSBY and JOHN HORNSBY

Chorus

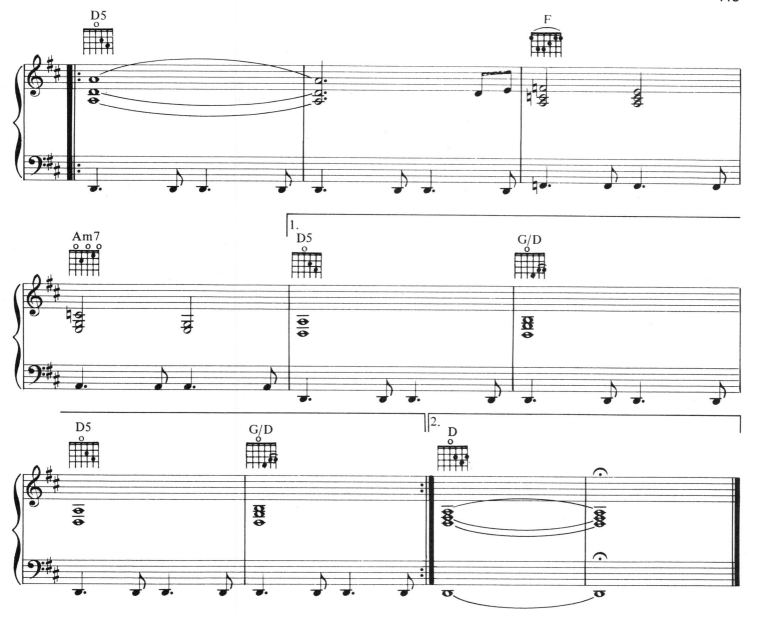

Additional Lyrics

2. She was proud and so strong
   And she tried not to listen to idle talk
   Downtown, where she walked.
   They sit around and they say
   That she came back with her tail between her legs,
   Like they always said she would.
   Well, I hear it's better on the other side.
   They say you'll never do it, so don't even try.
   Well, you may be beaten down with your closed mind,
   But don't try to make it mine. *(To Chorus)*

3. Standing on the shore she looks to the west with a look of longing
   To where the grass seems greener.
   There's a hard and a distant prize,
   It probably won't happen but I think I'll try.
   Well, even if it doesn't happen for me,
   It still beats hanging around here. *(To Chorus)*

LOST SOUL

Words and Music by
B.R. HORNSBY

Additional Lyrics

3. There was one day, oh, I can remember,
   He sat alone with a pencil in his hand.
   All day long he drew careful on the paper.
   In the end, just a picture of a man. *(To Chorus)*

4. Oh, dear Mary, do you remember
   The day when we went walking downtown?
   As I recall it was in early December
   After school had just let out.

5. When I see you on the street in the twilight,
   I may tip my hat and keep my head down.
   You show me love but maybe I don't deserve it.
   I've been called but not been found. *(To Chorus)*

Stranded On Easy Street

Words and Music by
B.R. HORNSBY and JOHN HORNSBY

might get strand-ed on Eas-y Street.

Additional Lyrics

2. Well, she said she was a good time girl,
   Laughing, laughing a bit too loud.
   Such a fine face, the specialist creates.
   She gets the benefit of the doubt.

2nd Pre-chorus: I know that she wanted more than I could give,
But I just had to see how the other half lived.
She showed me her friends, she showed me her throne.
I didn't sell my soul, I just took out a loan. *(To Chorus)*

3rd Pre-chorus: She runs to her mother, the social X-ray star.
She put me at the wheel of her father's new car.
She loved how her touch made me want to drive farther.
She loved how her money meant she'd tell me how far. *(To Chorus)*

Special Night

Words and Music
B.R. HORNSBY

126

Additional Lyrics

2. Looking out at the water,
   You say, "What do you think?"
   Indecision in my face and arms,
   You say, "You either swim or you sink".
   Sliding off, sliding on down,
   Wetness in the evening mist.
   No ride in the countryside
   Ever compared to this. *(To Chorus)*

STANDER ON THE MOUNTAIN

Words and Music by
B.R. HORNSBY

Moderately slow Rock

1. And he stands_ at the ban-quet room bar,____ look-ing
2. *See additional lyrics*

o-ver_ the crowd,_ the re-un-ion band play-ing too loud. And he sees_ his
3. *See additional lyrics*

fel-low old star, looks him up_ and down,_sees a lit-tle of him-self_ in his frown.

Chorus

The stand-er on the moun - tain,_ look - ing for the foun - tain to

drink some,_ to think some_ a - bout_ the old days._ King of the moun - tain,_

noth - ing could be found of the old ways,_ the old_ days_ when he_ was the one._

And the stand - er on the moun - tain runs.

130

131

The king of the hill runs a- way, now,

the king of the hill_ runs_ a-way.

Repeat and fade

Additional Lyrics

2. Let us sit and talk of old times,
   That's what we're supposed to do.
   And you don't look a day over thirty-two.
   Yes, we were so funny and wild.
   There's an old friend of mine
   Says I'm looking back most all the time.

2nd Chorus: The stander on the mountain
   Listens to the sounds of the city streets,
   The lonely beat of the town he once owned.
   King of the mountain,
   Nothing could be found of the old ways,
   The old days when he was the one.
   And the stander on the mountain runs. *(To Bridge)*

3. I recall when you filled it on up
   And you bowed to the crowd,
   The girls in short skirts screaming loud.

3rd Chorus: The stander on the mountain,
   Looking for the fountain to drink some,
   To think some about the old days.
   Big man around town,
   Nothing could be found of the old ways,
   The old days when he was the one. *(To Coda)*

A NIGHT ON THE TOWN

Words and Music by
B.R. HORNSBY and JOHN HORNSBY

134

Woh.

Chorus

Go - in' out for a night on the town,

go - in' out for a smoke and the trees.___ Go - in' out for a night on the town,

go - in' out for a look and see.___ Said - a, do what your dad - dy told___ you. Well, I

just went out___ and did that. Van___ and Wil - lie went - a out - a one night.___

Go -in' out   for a night   on the town,____

Repeat and fade

go -in' out for a night   on the town.____

Additional Lyrics

2. Well, there's a green table down at the Midway,
   Where they rack up the balls for games,
   And reputations are made.
   There's a green forest full of oaks and pines
   Where they cleared a space in the middle,
   Where secret scores are settled.

2nd Pre-chorus: And the claim was made round the table that night,
And they rode off through the trees.
And the young boys tell how the city boys tried,
And how one man fell to his knees.

2nd Chorus: Going out for a night on the town,
Going out for a smoke and the trees.
Going out for a night on the town,
Going out for a look and see.
Said, what made you go and do that?
Well, we were just having a little fun.
Van and Willie went out one night.

3rd Pre-chorus: And the line was drawn for another showdown
Like they's always seen and done.
And one night for a drunken old time
Left a scar on another one.

Repeat 1st Chorus

ANOTHER DAY

Words and Music by
B.R. HORNSBY

1. Woke up this morn - ing,
2.3.4. *See additional lyrics*

look - ing at the screen.

There's a cou - ple men talk - ing, I'm not so

sure_ what they mean.

There's a con - ver - sa - tion, man - y men_

run - ning wild.

We learn a - bout the world while they're

fight - ing in the aisles.__ Here we go.

Chorus

What do you say? What do you

know?

When you've got your life and you watch it a-

4th time to Coda I;
5th time to Coda II

way,

you got - ta say__ it's just an - oth - er

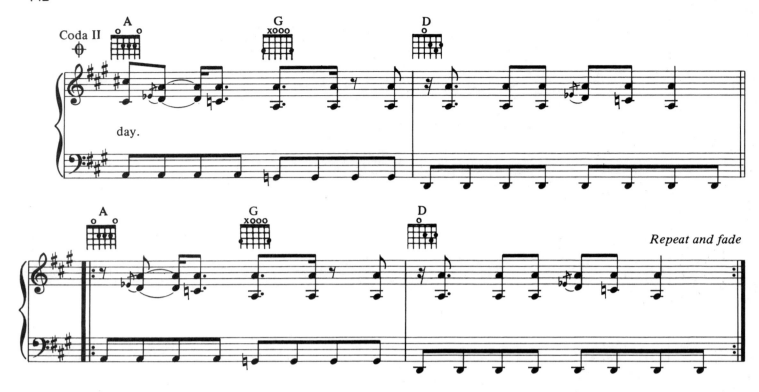

Repeat and fade

Additional Lyrics

2. Well, the Home Shopping Channel's got us by the eyes.
   Scrambling to the phone, ordering porcelain flies.
   Talk to the women, talk to the wives.
   Everybody's buying important things for their lives. *(To Chorus)*

3. He's a high performance engine with Jesus as the fuel.
   Old father's handing out forty acres and a mule.
   Preaching the word of prosperity,
   Make a little more money, they might just put you on TV. *(To Chorus)*

4. Turn off the lights, honey, then turn off the set.
   Life around here don't make a lot of damn sense.
   As I closed my eyes, I saw in my mind
   Somebody selling me a nickel for a dime. *(To Chorus)*

Carry The Water

Words and Music by
B.R. HORNSBY

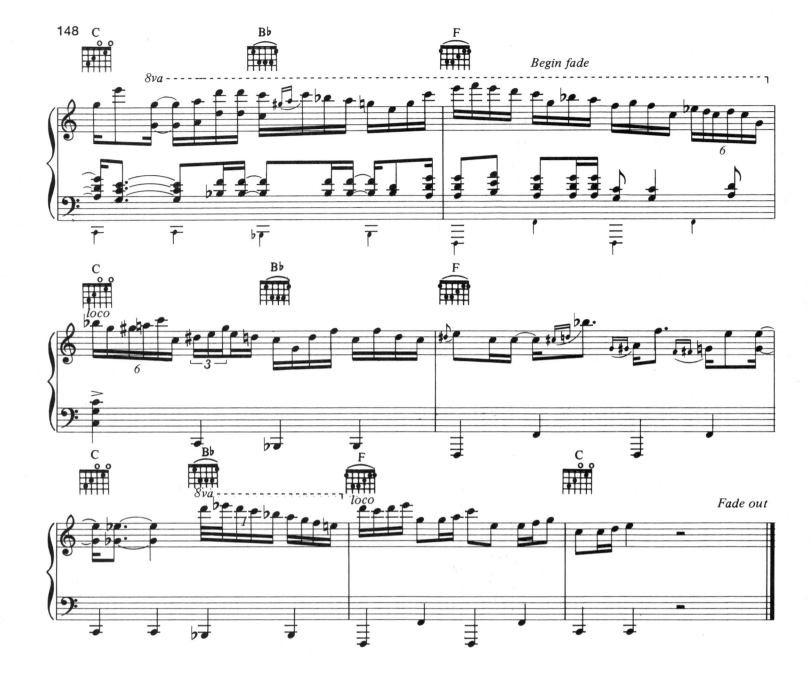

Additional Lyrics

2. Working hard, sweating all day in the long hot sun,
   Feel alone, with a heavy load, you're not the only one.
   Bossman says time to jump, we say how high.
   If you need a hand getting off your feet, baby I'll try.

2nd Pre-chorus: I want to cover you like the sea on the sand.
   Easy to be cynical, never take a stand.
   Easy for me not to give a damn.
   I'll ask you to call for me and I'll give you a hand. *(To Chorus)*

3rd Pre-chorus: Well, the lonely nights and lonley days,
   You wait for someone to come along and sweep you away.
   I'll put myself out there, it just might feel good.
   I don't always do that, but I think I should. *(To Chorus)*

Fire On The Cross

Words and Music by
B.R. HORNSBY and JOHN HORNSBY

1. They're look-in' for some hi-red guns__ on the Tex-as bor-
2. *See additional lyrics*

der,__ to shoot 'em all down if they try to cross o-ver the wa-ter.__ And they've

Additional Lyrics

2. There wasn't any sound, but it felt like sudden thunder.
   Two boards nailed together and burning bright.
   He was walking by the window when he saw it; now he wonders
   Just what he's got to do to make him see.
   He just wants to be brothers.
   The nights they came on horses, *etc.*

These Arms Of Mine

Words and Music by
B.R. HORNSBY

Additional Lyrics

2. Well, I'm walking the line
   Between wrong and right.
   I could go either way,
   But now you don't want me to stay.
   You're so tired of waiting.
   Well, I'm no saint.
   Tried to have my cake and eat it too.
   But nobody does what you do.
   Now another wins and I lose.
   I might deserve to. *(To Pre-chorus)*

BARREN GROUND

Words and Music by
B.R. HORNSBY and JOHN HORNSBY

Woh, where will you go?

What -'ll you do?

161

And the sons and the daugh-ters got dia-monds and gold. ___

But they were giv-en a land where strong ___ roots nev-er ___ take hold. ___

cresc.

Coda

mf

Repeat and fade

Additional Lyrics

2. There was a ship along the coast carrying a hold of black money
   In the sound near the northern lights.
   When the ship set sail, the crew looked for guidance
   In the bottom of an empty glass.
   Then the captain said, "Pour me another rye."
   Then the water turned black as that cold winter's night. *(To Chorus)*

Harbor Lights

Words and Music by
B.R. HORNSBY

(Guitar solo - 2nd time only)

D.S. 𝄉 al Coda ⊕

169

Talk Of The Town

Words and Music by
B.R. HORNSBY

I've been

ri - ding a - round with the top down, like I al - ways
sta - tue there in the town square seems to stare at

do,   my love at my side___ but on-ly this time my
me.   Walk-ing a-round___ with my head down, they

friends say some - thing's changed you.   They said you're run-ning with the
say can't we___ make you see.   Said, son, you know___ we're real-ly

wrong set,___ the girl is some-one you should nev-er have___ met.
col-or blind___ but ev-'ry-bod-y else seems to real-ly mind.

Bm11

Let her go on her own, son.___ Ev-'ry-one else has just
Lose her now, I think you'll find___ ev-'ry-thing else will just

174

talk of the town.

(Sax)

To Coda ✛ |1.

The

|2. N.C.

We're proba - bly not the first, we're

Long Tall Cool One

Words and Music by
B.R. HORNSBY

Is he sane___ or in - sane? That's - a all they want___ to know.
Walk-ing in___ the shad - ows, now I want back in the light.

China Doll

Words and Music by
B.R. HORNSBY

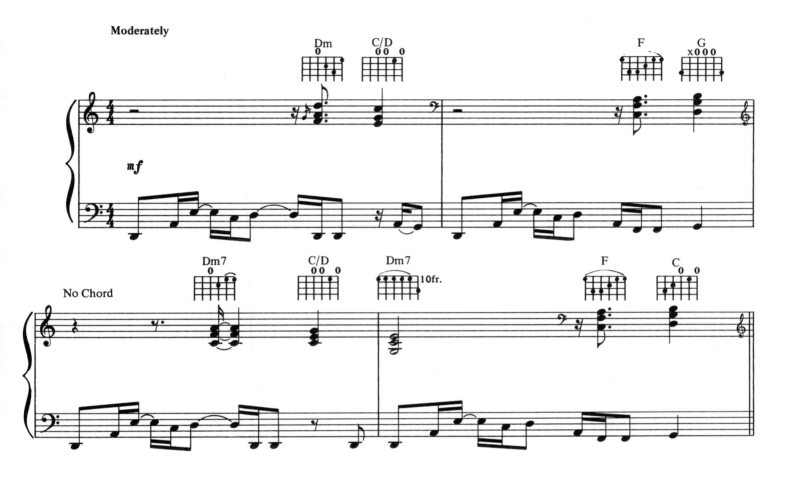

You lie o - ver there in a bed with iron _____ rails.
(See additional lyrics)

Bass simile throughout

help you get__ through.___   May not be much, but now it's all that I__ can do,___

down your wear - y head,___   do what-ev - er you got - ta do.
ease your wor - ried mind,_

do some-thing to get through. *(Guitar solo)*

In a world where you nev-er know. I'll be there for you,___ I'll be there___ for you.___

Repeat and fade (solo ad lib)

Additional lyrics

Put on your strong face when they're in the room
Can't show signs of weakness; an unspoken rule
Put on your strong face, act like nothing's wrong
We can be so helpless, helpless and so strong
(To Chorus)

Fields Of Gray

Words and Music by
B.R. HORNSBY

Moderately

When the

cross   the   fields   of __ gray. __

Rainbow's Cadillac

Words and Music by
B.R. HORNSBY

it down___ at the pro-per time.___ Ev-ery night___ a-bout a quar-ter to ten___ from the mid-dle of June___ to the sum-mer's end,___ peo-ple would gath-er from miles a-round___ to see the might-y Rain-bow knock 'em down.___ *(Horns)*

Repeat and fade (Instrumental solos)

Passing Through

Words and Music by
B.R. HORNSBY

209

The Tide Will Rise

Words by
B.R. HORNSBY and
JOHN HORNSBY

Music by
B.R. HORNSBY

213

WHAT A TIME

Words by
JOHN HORNSBY

Music by
B.R. HORNSBY

Moderately fast

Well, it came on fast when I heard the blast and the

main gen - er - a - tor made a gi - ant gasp,

it was 'round a - bout mid - night, , 'bout half past,

ci - ty went black as coal so fast.

Thou-sand peo - ple sing-in' in the dark, could-n't see a thing._____

Thou-sand peo - ple sing-in' in the dark. Whoa.

Whoa.

Whoa.

228

(Repeat for solos, ad lib)

Pastures Of Plenty

Words and Music by
B.R. HORNSBY

230

Repeat for solos (Play four times)

She looked down_____ the rail - road track,

lined with trees__ on each side.

The End Of The Innocence

Words and Music by
DON HENLEY and B.R. HORNSBY

Re - mem - ber when_ the days_
beau - ti - ful,_ for spac-
Who knows how_ long this_